Verses to Share

Perfect Bible Verses
for
Special Occasions

WORLD PUBLISHING

Grand Rapids, Michigan 49418 U.S.A.

Verses to Share
Copyright 1996 by World Publishing. All rights reserved.

Some of the Scripture readings in this book have been taken from The *Holy Bible*, King James Version.

Some of the Scripture readings in this book have been taken from *GOD'S WORD*, copyright 1995 by God's Word to the Nations Bible Society. All rights reserved. Used by permission.

GOD'S WORD uses half-brackets (⌊ ⌋) to enclose words that the translation team supplied because the context contains meaning that is not explicitly stated in the original language.

GOD'S WORD™ SERIES and its associated logo are trademarks of God's Word to the Nations Bible Society.

Up to 500 verses from GOD'S WORD may be quoted in any form (printed, written, visual, electronic, or audio) without written permission, provided that no more than half of any one book is quoted, and the verses quoted do not amount to more than 25% of the text of the work in which they are quoted. The designation (*GOD'S WORD*) must always appear after each quotation.

Developed and produced by The Livingstone Corporation. Project staff include: James C. Galvin, Christopher D. Hudson, Amber Rae Hudson, Brenda J. Todd.

Cover design by Paetzold Design.

ISBN 0-529-106957
Library of Congress Catalog Card Number 96-60871
Published by: World Publishing, Inc.
                 Grand Rapids, Michigan 49418 USA
                 All rights reserved.

Printed in the United States of America

1 2 3 4 5 6 7 00 99 98 97 96

Contents

Introduction	v	Graduation	62
Anniversary	1	Grandparent's Day	67
Baptism	5	Letter to Father or Mother	69
Bereavement	8	Letter to Son or Daughter	70
Bible Presentation	16	Mother's Day	77
Birth Announcement	22	New Year's	79
Birthday	24	Retirement	82
Boss's Day	27	Secretary's Day	85
Christmas	30	Thank You	87
Confirmation	33	Thanksgiving	90
Easter	37	Thinking of You	93
Encouragement	43	Valentine's Day	95
Father's Day	48	Wedding	99
Friendship	51	Verses for Other Occasions	106
Get Well	55	Dates to Remember	117
Good Friday	59		

Introduction

Have you ever struggled to find an appropriate Bible verse for a card or note that you are sending to someone special?

***Verses to Share** helps you find the right Scripture.* Hundreds of choice Bible passages are arranged by topic so you can find the perfect verse for that special occasion. Each verse is reprinted from the new, easy-to-read *GOD'S WORD* translation, as well as from the classic King James Version.

***Verses to Share** is easy to use.* Look up any noteworthy occasion. Whether it's a card, letter, or note for a Birthday, Get Well, Mother's Day, or Thinking of you, you will find numerous verses to help add meaning to your correspondence.

***Verses to Share** helps you remember important dates.* A special calendar gives you a place to keep track of holidays, birthdays, anniversaries, and other events you want to remember year-to-year.

Anniversary

Proverbs 5:18

Let your own fountain be blessed,
and enjoy the girl you married when you were young.

(GOD'S WORD)

Let thy fountain be blessed: and rejoice with the wife of thy youth.

(KING JAMES)

Proverbs 18:22

Whoever finds a wife finds something good
and has obtained favor from the LORD.

(GOD'S WORD)

Whoso findeth a wife findeth a good thing, and obtaineth favour of the LORD.

(KING JAMES)

Proverbs 19:14

Home and wealth are inherited from fathers,
but a sensible wife comes from the LORD.

(GOD'S WORD)

House and riches are the inheritance of fathers and a prudent wife is from the LORD.

(KING JAMES)

Proverbs 31:10

**Who can find a wife with a strong character?
She is worth far more than jewels.**

(GOD'S WORD)

Who can find a virtuous woman? for her price is far above rubies.

(KING JAMES)

Ecclesiastes 4:9

Two people are better than one because ⌊together⌋ they have a good reward for their hard work.

(GOD'S WORD)

Two are better than one; because they have a good reward for their labour.

(KING JAMES)

Song of Songs 4:9-10

**My bride, my sister, you have charmed me.
You have charmed me
   with a single glance from your eyes,
   with a single strand of your necklace.
How beautiful are your expressions of love, my bride, my sister!
How much better are your expressions of love than wine
   and the fragrance of your perfume than any spice.**

(GOD'S WORD)

Thou hast ravished my heart, my sister, my spouse; thou hast ravished my heart with one of thine eyes, with one chain of thy neck.

How fair is thy love, my sister, my spouse! how much better is thy love than wine! and the smell of thine ointments than all spices!

(KING JAMES)

Anniversary

Song of Songs 8:7a

**Raging water cannot extinguish love,
   and rivers will never wash it away.**

(GOD'S WORD)

Many waters cannot quench love, neither can the floods drown it.

(KING JAMES)

1 Corinthians 13:4-8a

**Love is patient. Love is kind. Love isn't jealous. It doesn't sing its
own praises. It isn't arrogant. It isn't rude. It doesn't think about
itself. It isn't irritable. It doesn't keep track of wrongs. It isn't
happy when injustice is done, but it is happy with the truth. Love
never stops being patient, never stops believing, never stops hoping, never gives up.**

   Love never comes to an end.

(GOD'S WORD)

Charity suffereth long, and is kind; charity envieth not; charity vaunteth not
itself, is not puffed up,

Doth not behave itself unseemly, seeketh not her own, is not easily
provoked, thinketh no evil;

Rejoiceth not in iniquity, but rejoiceth in the truth;

Beareth all things, believeth all things, hopeth all things, endureth all
things.

Charity never faileth.

(KING JAMES)

Anniversary

1 Corinthians 13:13

So these three things remain: faith, hope, and love. But the best one of these is love.

(GOD'S WORD)

And now abideth faith, hope, charity, these three; but the greatest of these is charity.

(KING JAMES)

Ephesians 5:31

That's why a man will leave his father and mother and be united with his wife, and the two will be one.

(GOD'S WORD)

For this cause shall a man leave his father and mother, and shall be joined unto his wife, and they two shall be one flesh.

(KING JAMES)

Ephesians 5:33

But every husband must love his wife as he loves himself, and wives should respect their husbands.

(GOD'S WORD)

Nevertheless let every one of you in particular so love his wife even as himself; and the wife see that she reverence her husband.

(KING JAMES)

Baptism

Colossians 3:18-19

Wives, place yourselves under your husbands' authority. This is appropriate behavior for the Lord's people. Husbands, love your wives, and don't be harsh with them.

(GOD'S WORD)

Wives, submit yourselves unto your own husbands, as it is fit in the Lord. Husbands, love your wives, and be not bitter against them.

(KING JAMES)

Baptism

Psalm 111:10

The fear of the LORD is the beginning of wisdom.
Good sense is shown by everyone
who follows ⌊God's guiding principles⌋.
His praise continues forever.

(GOD'S WORD)

The fear of the LORD is the beginning of wisdom: a good understanding have all they that do his commandments: his praise endureth for ever.

(KING JAMES)

5

Baptism

Mark 16:16a
Whoever believes and is baptized will be saved.

(GOD'S WORD)

He that believeth and is baptized shall be saved.

(KING JAMES)

Romans 6:4
When we were baptized into his death, we were placed into the tomb with him. As Christ was brought back from death to life by the glorious power of the Father, so we, too, should live a new kind of life.

(GOD'S WORD)

Therefore we are buried with him by baptism into death: that like as Christ was raised up from the dead by the glory of the Father, even so we also should walk in newness of life.

(KING JAMES)

1 Corinthians 12:13
By one Spirit we were all baptized into one body. Whether we are Jewish or Greek, slave or free, God gave all of us one Spirit to drink.

(GOD'S WORD)

For by one Spirit are we all baptized into one body, whether we be Jews or Gentiles, whether we be bond or free; and have been all made to drink into one Spirit.

(KING JAMES)

Baptism

2 Corinthians 5:17

Whoever is a believer in Christ is a new creation. The old way of living has disappeared. A new way of living has come into existence.

(GOD'S WORD)

Therefore if any man be in Christ, he is a new creature: old things are passed away; behold, all things are become new.

(KING JAMES)

Galatians 3:27

Clearly, all of you who were baptized in Christ's name have clothed yourselves with Christ.

(GOD'S WORD)

For as many of you as have been baptized into Christ have put on Christ.

(KING JAMES)

Ephesians 4:5-6

There is one Lord, one faith, one baptism, one God and Father of all, who is over everything, through everything, and in everything.

(GOD'S WORD)

One Lord, one faith, one baptism,
One God and Father of all, who is above all, and through all, and in you all.

(KING JAMES)

Bereavement

Psalm 20:1
The LORD will answer you in times of trouble.
The name of the God of Jacob will protect you.

(GOD'S WORD)

The LORD hear thee in the day of trouble; the name of the God of Jacob defend thee.

(KING JAMES)

Psalm 27:14
Wait with hope for the LORD.
Be strong, and let your heart be courageous.
Yes, wait with hope for the LORD.

(GOD'S WORD)

Wait on the LORD: be of good courage, and he shall strengthen thine heart: wait, I say, on the LORD.

(KING JAMES)

Psalm 34:18
The LORD is near to those whose hearts are humble.
He saves those whose spirits are crushed.

(GOD'S WORD)

Bereavement

The LORD is nigh unto them that are of a broken heart; and saveth such as be of a contrite spirit.

(KING JAMES)

Psalm 42:5

Why are you discouraged, my soul?
Why are you so restless?
 Put your hope in God,
  because I will still praise him.
   He is my savior and my God.

(GOD'S WORD)

Why art thou cast down, O my soul? and why art thou disquieted in me? hope thou in God: for I shall yet praise him for the help of his countenance.

(KING JAMES)

Psalm 54:4

God is my helper!
The Lord is the provider for my life.

(GOD'S WORD)

Behold, God is mine helper: the Lord is with them that uphold my soul.

(KING JAMES)

Psalm 55:22

Turn your burdens over to the LORD,
 and he will take care of you.
  He will never let the righteous person stumble.

(GOD'S WORD)

Bereavement

Cast thy burden upon the LORD, and he shall sustain thee: he shall never suffer the righteous to be moved.

(KING JAMES)

Psalm 68:5

**The God who is in his holy dwelling place
is the father of the fatherless and the defender of widows.**

(GOD'S WORD)

A father of the fatherless, and a judge of the widows, is God in his holy habitation.

(KING JAMES)

Psalm 68:19

**Thanks be to the Lord,
who daily carries our burdens for us.
God is our salvation.**

(GOD'S WORD)

Blessed be the Lord, who daily loadeth us with benefits, even the God of our salvation.

(KING JAMES)

Psalm 116:7

**Be at peace again, my soul,
because the LORD has been good to you.**

(GOD'S WORD)

Return unto thy rest, O my soul; for the LORD hath dealt bountifully with thee.

(KING JAMES)

Bereavement

Psalm 116:15

**Precious in the sight of the LORD
is the death of his faithful ones.**

(GOD'S WORD)

Precious in the sight of the LORD is the death of his saints.

(KING JAMES)

Lamentations 3:25-26

**The LORD is good to those who wait for him,
to anyone who seeks help from him.**

**"It is good to continue to hope and wait silently
for the LORD to save us."**

(GOD'S WORD)

The LORD is good unto them that wait for him, to the soul that seeketh him.
It is good that a man should both hope and quietly wait for the salvation of
the LORD.

(KING JAMES)

Matthew 5:4

**Blessed are those who mourn.
They will be comforted.**

(GOD'S WORD)

Blessed are they that mourn: for they shall be comforted.

(KING JAMES)

1 Corinthians 15:53-55

This body that decays must be changed into a body that cannot decay. This mortal body must be changed into a body that will live forever. When this body that decays is changed into a body that cannot decay, and this mortal body is changed into a body that will live forever, then the teaching of Scripture will come true:

"Death is turned into victory!
Death, where is your victory?
Death, where is your sting?"

(GOD'S WORD)

For this corruptible must put on incorruption, and this mortal must put on immortality.

So when this corruptible shall have put on incorruption, and this mortal shall have put on immortality, then shall be brought to pass the saying that is written, Death is swallowed up in victory.

O death, where is thy sting? O grave, where is thy victory?

(KING JAMES)

2 Corinthians 1:3-5

Praise the God and Father of our Lord Jesus Christ! He is the Father who is compassionate and the God who gives comfort. He comforts us whenever we suffer. That is why whenever other people suffer, we are able to comfort them by using the same comfort we have received from God. Because Christ suffered so much for us, we can receive so much comfort from him.

(GOD'S WORD)

Blessed be God, even the Father of our Lord Jesus Christ, the Father of mercies, and the God of all comfort;

Who comforteth us in all our tribulation, that we may be able to comfort them which are in any trouble, by the comfort wherewith we ourselves are comforted of God.

For as the sufferings of Christ abound in us, so our consolation also aboundeth by Christ.

(KING JAMES)

2 Corinthians 4:16-18

That is why we are not discouraged. Though outwardly we are wearing out, inwardly we are renewed day by day. Our suffering is light and temporary and is producing for us an eternal glory that is greater than anything we can imagine. We don't look for things that can be seen but for things that can't be seen. Things that can be seen are only temporary. But things that can't be seen last forever.

(GOD'S WORD)

For which cause we faint not; but though our outward man perish, yet the inward man is renewed day by day.

For our light affliction, which is but for a moment, worketh for us a far more exceeding and eternal weight of glory;

While we look not at the things which are seen, but at the things which are not seen: for the things which are seen are temporal; but the things which are not seen are eternal.

(KING JAMES)

Bereavement

2 Corinthians 5:1

We know that if the life we live here on earth is ever taken down like a tent, we still have a building from God. It is an eternal house in heaven that isn't made by human hands.

(GOD'S WORD)

For we know that if our earthly house of this tabernacle were dissolved, we have a building of God, an house not made with hands, eternal in the heavens.

(KING JAMES)

Philippians 1:21

Christ means everything to me in this life, and when I die I'll have even more.

(GOD'S WORD)

For to me to live is Christ, and to die is gain.

(KING JAMES)

1 Thessalonians 4:13-14

Brothers and sisters, we don't want you to be ignorant about those who have died. We don't want you to grieve like other people who have no hope. We believe that Jesus died and came back to life. We also believe that, through Jesus, God will bring back those who have died. They will come back with Jesus.

(GOD'S WORD)

Bereavement

But I would not have you to be ignorant, brethren, concerning them which are asleep, that ye sorrow not, even as others which have no hope.

For if we believe that Jesus died and rose again, even so them also which sleep in Jesus will God bring with him.

(KING JAMES)

1 Peter 5:10

God, who shows you his kindness and who has called you through Christ Jesus to his eternal glory, will restore you, strengthen you, make you strong, and support you as you suffer for a little while.

(GOD'S WORD)

But the God of all grace, who hath called us unto his eternal glory by Christ Jesus, after that ye have suffered a while, make you perfect, stablish, strengthen, settle you.

(KING JAMES)

Revelation 21:3-4

I heard a loud voice from the throne say, "God lives with humans! God will make his home with them, and they will be his people. God himself will be with them and be their God. He will wipe every tear from their eyes. There won't be any more death. There won't be any grief, crying, or pain, because the first things have disappeared."

(GOD'S WORD)

Bereavement

And I heard a great voice out of heaven saying, Behold, the tabernacle of God is with men, and he will dwell with them, and they shall be his people, and God himself shall be with them, and be their God.

And God shall wipe away all tears from their eyes; and there shall be no more death, neither sorrow, nor crying, neither shall there be any more pain: for the former things are passed away.

(KING JAMES)

Bible Presentation

Joshua 1:8

Never stop reciting these teachings. You must think about them night and day so that you will faithfully do everything written in them. Only then will you prosper and succeed.

(GOD'S WORD)

This book of the law shall not depart out of thy mouth; but thou shalt meditate therein day and night, that thou mayest observe to do according to all that is written therein: for then thou shalt make thy way prosperous, and then thou shalt have good success.

(KING JAMES)

Joshua 22:5

Carefully follow the commands and teachings that the LORD's servant Moses gave you. Love the LORD your God, follow his directions, and keep his commands. Be loyal to him, and serve him with all your heart and soul.

(GOD'S WORD)

But take diligent heed to do the commandment and the law, which Moses the servant of the LORD charged you, to love the LORD your God, and to walk in all his ways, and to keep his commandments, and to cleave unto him, and to serve him with all your heart and with all your soul.

(KING JAMES)

1 Samuel 15:22

Then Samuel said,

**"Is the LORD as delighted with burnt offerings and sacrifices
as he would be with your obedience?
To follow instructions is better than to sacrifice.
To obey is better than sacrificing the fat of rams."**

(GOD'S WORD)

And Samuel said, Hath the LORD as great delight in burnt offerings and sacrifices, as in obeying the voice of the LORD? Behold, to obey is better than sacrifice, and to hearken than the fat of rams.

(KING JAMES)

Bible Presentation

2 Samuel 22:31

God's way is perfect!
  The promise of the LORD has proven to be true.
  He is a shield to all those who take refuge in him.

(GOD'S WORD)

As for God, his way is perfect; the word of the LORD is tried: he is a buckler to all them that trust in him.

(KING JAMES)

1 Chronicles 16:11

Search for the LORD and his strength.
Always seek his presence.

(GOD'S WORD)

Seek the LORD and his strength, seek his face continually.

(KING JAMES)

Psalm 19:7-8

The teachings of the LORD are perfect.
  They renew the soul.
The testimony of the LORD is dependable.
  It makes gullible people wise.
The instructions of the LORD are correct.
  They make the heart rejoice.
The command of the LORD is radiant.
  It makes the eyes shine.

(GOD'S WORD)

The law of the LORD is perfect, converting the soul: the testimony of the LORD is sure, making wise the simple.

The statutes of the LORD are right, rejoicing the heart: the commandment of the LORD is pure, enlightening the eyes.

(KING JAMES)

Psalm 111:10

The fear of the LORD is the beginning of wisdom.
Good sense is shown by everyone
who follows ₁God's guiding principles₁.
His praise continues forever.

(GOD'S WORD)

The fear of the LORD is the beginning of wisdom: a good understanding have all they that do his commandments: his praise endureth for ever.

(KING JAMES)

Psalm 112:1

Hallelujah!

Blessed is the person who fears the LORD
and is happy to obey his commands.

(GOD'S WORD)

Praise ye the LORD. Blessed is the man that feareth the LORD, that delighteth greatly in his commandments.

(KING JAMES)

Bible Presentation

Psalm 119:18

**Uncover my eyes
so that I may see the miraculous things in your teachings.**
(GOD'S WORD)

Open thou mine eyes, that I may behold wondrous things out of thy law.
(KING JAMES)

Psalm 119:165

**There is lasting peace for those who love your teachings.
Nothing can make those people stumble.**
(GOD'S WORD)

Great peace have they which love thy law: and nothing shall offend them.
(KING JAMES)

Romans 15:4

**Everything written long ago was written to teach us so that we
would have confidence through the endurance and encouragement
which the Scriptures give us.**
(GOD'S WORD)

For whatsoever things were written aforetime were written for our
learning, that we through patience and comfort of the scriptures might
have hope.

(KING JAMES)

Bible Presentation

2 Timothy 3:16-17

Every Scripture passage is inspired by God. All of them are useful for teaching, pointing out errors, correcting people, and training them for a life that has God's approval. They equip God's servants so that they are completely prepared to do good things.

(GOD'S WORD)

All scripture is given by inspiration of God, and is profitable for doctrine, for reproof, for correction, for instruction in righteousness:

That the man of God may be perfect, throughly furnished unto all good works.

(KING JAMES)

Hebrews 4:12

God's word is living and active. It is sharper than any two-edged sword and cuts as deep as the place where soul and spirit meet, the place where joints and marrow meet. God's word judges a person's thoughts and intentions.

(GOD'S WORD)

For the word of God is quick, and powerful, and sharper than any two-edged sword, piercing even to the dividing asunder of soul and spirit, and of the joints and marrow, and is a discerner of the thoughts and intents of the heart.

(KING JAMES)

Birth Announcement

Psalm 127:4

**The children born to a man when he is young
  are like arrows in the hand of a warrior.**

(GOD'S WORD)

As arrows are in the hand of a mighty man; so are children of the youth.
(KING JAMES)

Psalm 139:13-16

**You alone created my inner being.
You knitted me together inside my mother.
I will give thanks to you
  because I have been so amazingly and miraculously made.
    Your works are miraculous, and my soul is fully aware of this.
My bones were not hidden from you
  when I was being made in secret,
  when I was being skillfully woven in an underground workshop.
Your eyes saw me when I was only a fetus.
  Every day ⌊of my life⌋ was recorded in your book
    before one of them had taken place.**

(GOD'S WORD)

Birth Announcement

For thou hast possessed my reins: thou hast covered me in my mother's womb.

I will praise thee; for I am fearfully and wonderfully made: marvellous are thy works; and that my soul knoweth right well.

My substance was not hid from thee, when I was made in secret, and curiously wrought in the lowest parts of the earth.

Thine eyes did see my substance, yet being unperfect; and in thy book all my members were written, which in continuance were fashioned, when as yet there was none of them.

(KING JAMES)

Proverbs 22:6

Train a child in the way he should go,
  and even when he is old he will not turn away from it.

(GOD'S WORD)

Train up a child in the way he should go: and when he is old, he will not depart from it.

(KING JAMES)

Proverbs 23:24-25

A righteous person's father will certainly rejoice.
Someone who has a wise son will enjoy him.
  May your father and your mother be glad.
  May she who gave birth to you rejoice.

(GOD'S WORD)

The father of the righteous shall greatly rejoice: and he that begetteth a wise child shall have joy of him.

Thy father and thy mother shall be glad, and she that bare thee shall rejoice.

(KING JAMES)

Matthew 18:4

Whoever becomes like this little child is the greatest in the kingdom of heaven.

(GOD'S WORD)

Whosoever therefore shall humble himself as this little child, the same is greatest in the kingdom of heaven.

(KING JAMES)

Birthday

Psalm 22:10

I was placed in your care from birth.
  From my mother's womb you have been my God.

(GOD'S WORD)

I was cast upon thee from the womb: thou art my God from my mother's belly.

(KING JAMES)

Birthday

Psalm 71:6

I depended on you before I was born.
You took me from my mother's womb.
My songs of praise constantly speak about you.

(GOD'S WORD)

By thee have I been holden up from the womb: thou art he that took me out of my mother's bowels: my praise shall be continually of thee.

(KING JAMES)

Psalm 90:12

Teach us to number each of our days
so that we may grow in wisdom.

(GOD'S WORD)

So teach us to number our days, that we may apply our hearts unto wisdom.

(KING JAMES)

Psalm 139:16

Your eyes saw me when I was only a fetus.
Every day ⌊of my life⌋ was recorded in your book
before one of them had taken place.

(GOD'S WORD)

Thine eyes did see my substance, yet being unperfect; and in thy book all my members were written, which in continuance were fashioned, when as yet there was none of them.

(KING JAMES)

Birthday

Isaiah 49:1b

Before I was born, the LORD chose me.
While I was in my mother's womb, he recorded my name.

(GOD'S WORD)

The LORD hath called me from the womb; from the bowels of my mother hath he made mention of my name.

(KING JAMES)

Jeremiah 1:5

Before I formed you in the womb,
  I knew you.
Before you were born,
  I set you apart for my holy purpose.
  I appointed you to be a prophet to the nations.

(GOD'S WORD)

Before I formed thee in the belly I knew thee; and before thou camest forth out of the womb I sanctified thee, and I ordained thee a prophet unto the nations.

(KING JAMES)

Jeremiah 29:11

I know the plans that I have for you, declares the LORD. They are plans for peace and not disaster, plans to give you a future filled with hope.

(GOD'S WORD)

For I know the thoughts that I think toward you, saith the LORD, thoughts of peace, and not of evil, to give you an expected end.

(KING JAMES)

Boss's Day

1 Chronicles 16:11

Search for the LORD and his strength.
Always seek his presence.

(GOD'S WORD)

Seek the LORD and his strength, seek his face continually.

(KING JAMES)

Psalm 111:10

The fear of the LORD is the beginning of wisdom.
Good sense is shown by everyone
who follows ₍God's guiding principles₎.
His praise continues forever.

(GOD'S WORD)

The fear of the LORD is the beginning of wisdom: a good understanding
have all they that do his commandments: his praise endureth for ever.

(KING JAMES)

Boss's Day

Psalm 112:1

Hallelujah!

**Blessed is the person who fears the LORD
and is happy to obey his commands.**

(GOD'S WORD)

Praise ye the LORD. Blessed is the man that feareth the LORD, that delighteth greatly in his commandments.

(KING JAMES)

Psalm 119:165

**There is lasting peace for those who love your teachings.
Nothing can make those people stumble.**

(GOD'S WORD)

Great peace have they which love thy law: and nothing shall offend them.

(KING JAMES)

Proverbs 3:5-6

**Trust the LORD with all your heart,
and do not rely on your own understanding.
In all your ways acknowledge him,
and he will make your paths smooth.**

(GOD'S WORD)

Trust in the LORD with all thine heart; and lean not unto thine own understanding.

In all thy ways acknowledge him, and he shall direct thy paths.

(KING JAMES)

Boss's Day

Proverbs 16:3

**Entrust your efforts to the LORD,
and your plans will succeed.**

(GOD'S WORD)

Commit thy works unto the LORD, and thy thoughts shall be established.

(KING JAMES)

Colossians 3:17

**Everything you say or do should be done in the name of the Lord
Jesus, giving thanks to God the Father through him.**

(GOD'S WORD)

And whatsoever ye do in word or deed, do all in the name of the Lord
Jesus, giving thanks to God and the Father by him.

(KING JAMES)

Colossians 3:23

**Whatever you do, do it wholeheartedly as though you were working
for your real master and not merely for humans.**

(GOD'S WORD)

And whatsoever ye do, do it heartily, as to the Lord, and not unto men.

(KING JAMES)

Christmas

Isaiah 7:14

So the Lord himself will give you this sign: A virgin will become pregnant and give birth to a son, and she will name him Immanuel [God Is With Us].

(GOD'S WORD)

Therefore the Lord himself shall give you a sign; Behold, a virgin shall conceive, and bear a son, and shall call his name Immanuel.

(KING JAMES)

Isaiah 9:6

A child will be born for us.
A son will be given to us.
The government will rest on his shoulders.
He will be named:
Wonderful Counselor,
Mighty God,
Everlasting Father,
Prince of Peace.

(GOD'S WORD)

Christmas

For unto us a child is born, unto us a son is given: and the government shall be upon his shoulder: and his name shall be called Wonderful, Counsellor, The mighty God, The everlasting Father, The Prince of Peace.

(KING JAMES)

Isaiah 28:16

This is what the Almighty LORD says:

> **I am going to lay a rock in Zion,**
> **a rock that has been tested,**
> **a precious cornerstone,**
> **a solid foundation.**
> **Whoever believes ₍in him₎ will not worry.**

(GOD'S WORD)

Therefore thus saith the Lord GOD, Behold, I lay in Zion for a foundation a stone, a tried stone, a precious corner stone, a sure foundation: he that believeth shall not make haste.

(KING JAMES)

Luke 1:32-33

He will be a great man
> **and will be called the Son of the Most High.**
The Lord God will give him
> **the throne of his ancestor David.**
Your son will be king of Jacob's people forever,
> **and his kingdom will never end.**

(GOD'S WORD)

He shall be great, and shall be called the Son of the Highest: and the Lord God shall give unto him the throne of his father David:

And he shall reign over the house of Jacob for ever; and of his kingdom there shall be no end.

(KING JAMES)

Luke 2:11

Today your Savior, Christ the Lord, was born in David's city.

(GOD'S WORD)

For unto you is born this day in the city of David a Saviour, which is Christ the Lord.

(KING JAMES)

Luke 2:14

**Glory to God in the highest heaven,
  and on earth peace to those who have his good will!**

(GOD'S WORD)

Glory to God in the highest, and on earth peace, good will toward men.

(KING JAMES)

John 1:14

The Word became human and lived among us. We saw his glory. It was the glory that the Father shares with his only Son, a glory full of kindness and truth.

(GOD'S WORD)

And the Word was made flesh, and dwelt among us, (and we beheld his glory, the glory as of the only begotten of the Father,) full of grace and truth.

(KING JAMES)

Confirmation

2 Samuel 22:31

God's way is perfect!
  The promise of the LORD has proven to be true.
    He is a shield to all those who take refuge in him.

(GOD'S WORD)

As for God, his way is perfect; the word of the LORD is tried: he is a buckler to all them that trust in him.

(KING JAMES)

Psalm 90:12

Teach us to number each of our days
  so that we may grow in wisdom.

(GOD'S WORD)

So teach us to number our days, that we may apply our hearts unto wisdom.

(KING JAMES)

Psalm 143:10

Teach me to do your will, because you are my God.
May your good Spirit lead me on level ground.

(GOD'S WORD)

Confirmation

Teach me to do thy will; for thou art my God: thy spirit is good; lead me into the land of uprightness.

(KING JAMES)

Proverbs 3:5-6

Trust the LORD with all your heart,
  and do not rely on your own understanding.
In all your ways acknowledge him,
  and he will make your paths smooth.

(GOD'S WORD)

Trust in the LORD with all thine heart; and lean not unto thine own understanding.

In all thy ways acknowledge him, and he shall direct thy paths.

(KING JAMES)

Proverbs 4:23

Guard your heart more than anything else,
  because the source of your life flows from it.

(GOD'S WORD)

Keep thy heart with all diligence; for out of it are the issues of life.

(KING JAMES)

Proverbs 22:6

Train a child in the way he should go,
  and even when he is old he will not turn away from it.

(GOD'S WORD)

Train up a child in the way he should go: and when he is old, he will not depart from it.

(KING JAMES)

Confirmation

Jeremiah 29:11

I know the plans that I have for you, declares the LORD. They are plans for peace and not disaster, plans to give you a future filled with hope.

(GOD'S WORD)

For I know the thoughts that I think toward you, saith the LORD, thoughts of peace, and not of evil, to give you an expected end.

(KING JAMES)

Hosea 6:3

Let's learn about the LORD.
Let's get to know the LORD.
   He will come to us as sure as the morning comes.
   He will come to us like the autumn rains and the spring rains
      that water the ground.

(GOD'S WORD)

Then shall we know, if we follow on to know the LORD: his going forth is prepared as the morning; and he shall come unto us as the rain, as the latter and former rain unto the earth.

(KING JAMES)

1 Corinthians 1:8-9

He will continue to give you strength until the end so that no one can accuse you of anything on the day of our Lord Jesus Christ. God faithfully keeps his promises. He called you to be partners with his Son Jesus Christ our Lord.

(GOD'S WORD)

Who shall also confirm you unto the end, that ye may be blameless in the day of our Lord Jesus Christ.

God is faithful, by whom ye were called unto the fellowship of his Son Jesus Christ our Lord.

(KING JAMES)

Colossians 2:6-7

You received Christ Jesus the Lord, so continue to live as Christ's people. Sink your roots in him and build on him. Be strengthened by the faith that you were taught, and overflow with thanksgiving.

(GOD'S WORD)

As ye have therefore received Christ Jesus the Lord, so walk ye in him:

Rooted and built up in him, and stablished in the faith, as ye have been taught, abounding therein with thanksgiving.

(KING JAMES)

2 Timothy 3:14-15

However, continue in what you have learned and found to be true. You know who your teachers were. From infancy you have known the Holy Scriptures. They have the power to give you wisdom so that you can be saved through faith in Christ Jesus.

(GOD'S WORD)

But continue thou in the things which thou hast learned and hast been assured of, knowing of whom thou hast learned them;

And that from a child thou hast known the holy scriptures, which are able to make thee wise unto salvation through faith which is in Christ Jesus.

(KING JAMES)

Easter

Isaiah 28:16

This is what the Almighty LORD says:

I am going to lay a rock in Zion,
a rock that has been tested,
a precious cornerstone,
a solid foundation.
Whoever believes ⌊in him⌋ will not worry.

(GOD'S WORD)

Therefore thus saith the Lord GOD, Behold, I lay in Zion for a foundation a stone, a tried stone, a precious corner stone, a sure foundation: he that believeth shall not make haste.

(KING JAMES)

Isaiah 53:5

He was wounded for our rebellious acts.
He was crushed for our sins.
He was punished so that we could have peace,
and we received healing from his wounds.

(GOD'S WORD)

But he was wounded for our transgressions, he was bruised for our iniquities: the chastisement of our peace was upon him; and with his stripes we are healed.

(KING JAMES)

Isaiah 53:10

Yet, it was the LORD's will to crush him with suffering. When the LORD has made his life a sacrifice for our wrongdoings, he will see his descendants for many days. The will of the LORD will succeed through him.

(GOD'S WORD)

Yet it pleased the LORD to bruise him; he hath put him to grief: when thou shalt make his soul an offering for sin, he shall see his seed, he shall prolong his days, and the pleasure of the LORD shall prosper in his hand.

(KING JAMES)

Matthew 28:5-6

The angel said to the women, "Don't be afraid! I know you're looking for Jesus, who was crucified. He's not here. He has been brought back to life as he said. Come, see the place where he was lying."

(GOD'S WORD)

And the angel answered and said unto the women, Fear not ye: for I know that ye seek Jesus, which was crucified.

He is not here: for he is risen, as he said. Come, see the place where the Lord lay.

(KING JAMES)

Mark 16:6

The young man said to them, "Don't panic! You're looking for Jesus from Nazareth, who was crucified. He has been brought back to life. He's not here. Look at the place where they laid him."

(GOD'S WORD)

And he saith unto them, Be not affrighted: Ye seek Jesus of Nazareth, which was crucified: he is risen; he is not here: behold the place where they laid him.

(KING JAMES)

Luke 18:31-33

Jesus took the twelve apostles aside and said to them, "We're going to Jerusalem. Everything that the prophets wrote about the Son of Man will come true. He will be handed over to foreigners. They will make fun of him, insult him, spit on him, whip him, and kill him. But on the third day he will come back to life."

(GOD'S WORD)

Then he took unto him the twelve, and said unto them, Behold, we go up to Jerusalem, and all things that are written by the prophets concerning the Son of man shall be accomplished.

For he shall be delivered unto the Gentiles, and shall be mocked, and spitefully entreated, and spitted on:

And they shall scourge him, and put him to death: and the third day he shall rise again.

(KING JAMES)

Luke 24:39

Look at my hands and feet, and see that it's really me. Touch me, and see for yourselves. Ghosts don't have flesh and bones, but you can see that I do.

(GOD'S WORD)

Behold my hands and my feet, that it is I myself: handle me, and see; for a spirit hath not flesh and bones, as ye see me have.

(KING JAMES)

Luke 24:46-47

He said to them, "Scripture says that the Messiah would suffer and that he would come back to life on the third day. Scripture also says that by the authority of Jesus people must be told to turn to God and change the way they think and act so that their sins will be forgiven. This must be told to people from all nations, beginning in the city of Jerusalem."

(GOD'S WORD)

And said unto them, Thus it is written, and thus it behoved Christ to suffer, and to rise from the dead the third day:

And that repentance and remission of sins should be preached in his name among all nations, beginning at Jerusalem.

(KING JAMES)

1 Corinthians 6:14

God raised the Lord, and by his power God will also raise us.

(GOD'S WORD)

And God hath both raised up the Lord, and will also raise up us by his own power.

(KING JAMES)

1 Corinthians 15:21-22

Since a man brought death, a man also brought life back from death. As everyone dies because of Adam, so also everyone will be made alive because of Christ.

(GOD'S WORD)

For since by man came death, by man came also the resurrection of the dead.

For as in Adam all die, even so in Christ shall all be made alive.

(KING JAMES)

2 Corinthians 5:21

God had Christ, who was sinless, take our sin so that we might receive God's approval through him.

(GOD'S WORD)

For he hath made him to be sin for us, who knew no sin; that we might be made the righteousness of God in him.

(KING JAMES)

Hebrews 2:9

Jesus was made a little lower than the angels, but we see him crowned with glory and honor because he suffered death. Through God's kindness he died on behalf of everyone.

(GOD'S WORD)

But we see Jesus, who was made a little lower than the angels for the suffering of death, crowned with glory and honour; that he by the grace of God should taste death for every man.

(KING JAMES)

Hebrews 9:28

Likewise, Christ was sacrificed once to take away the sins of humanity, and after that he will appear a second time. This time he will not deal with sin, but he will save those who eagerly wait for him.

(GOD'S WORD)

So Christ was once offered to bear the sins of many; and unto them that look for him shall he appear the second time without sin unto salvation.

(KING JAMES)

1 Peter 1:18-19

Realize that you weren't set free from the worthless life handed down to you from your ancestors by a payment of silver or gold which can be destroyed. Rather, the payment that freed you was the precious blood of Christ, the lamb with no defects or imperfections.

(GOD'S WORD)

Forasmuch as ye know that ye were not redeemed with corruptible things, as silver and gold, from your vain conversation received by tradition from your fathers;

But with the precious blood of Christ, as of a lamb without blemish and without spot.

(KING JAMES)

Encouragement

Joshua 23:14

Pay attention, because I will soon die like everyone else. You know with all your heart and soul that not one single promise which the LORD your God has given you has ever failed to come true. Every single word has come true.

(GOD'S WORD)

And, behold, this day I am going the way of all the earth: and ye know in all your hearts and in all your souls, that not one thing hath failed of all the good things which the LORD your God spake concerning you; all are come to pass unto you, and not one thing hath failed thereof.

(KING JAMES)

Psalm 34:18

**The LORD is near to those whose hearts are humble.
He saves those whose spirits are crushed.**

(GOD'S WORD)

The LORD is nigh unto them that are of a broken heart; and saveth such as be of a contrite spirit.

(KING JAMES)

Encouragement

Psalm 42:5

Why are you discouraged, my soul?
Why are you so restless?
  Put your hope in God,
    because I will still praise him.
      He is my savior and my God.

(GOD'S WORD)

Why art thou cast down, O my soul? and why art thou disquieted in me?
hope thou in God: for I shall yet praise him for the help of his countenance.

(KING JAMES)

Psalm 55:22

Turn your burdens over to the LORD,
  and he will take care of you.
    He will never let the righteous person stumble.

(GOD'S WORD)

Cast thy burden upon the LORD, and he shall sustain thee: he shall never
suffer the righteous to be moved.

(KING JAMES)

Psalm 68:19

Thanks be to the Lord,
  who daily carries our burdens for us.
    God is our salvation.

(GOD'S WORD)

Blessed be the Lord, who daily loadeth us with benefits, even the God of
our salvation.

(KING JAMES)

Encouragement

Psalm 116:7

**Be at peace again, my soul,
  because the Lord has been good to you.**

(GOD'S WORD)

Return unto thy rest, O my soul; for the Lord hath dealt bountifully with thee.

(KING JAMES)

Psalm 119:165

**There is lasting peace for those who love your teachings.
  Nothing can make those people stumble.**

(GOD'S WORD)

Great peace have they which love thy law: and nothing shall offend them.

(KING JAMES)

Psalm 145:17

**The Lord is fair in all his ways
  and faithful in everything he does.**

(GOD'S WORD)

The Lord is righteous in all his ways, and holy in all his works.

(KING JAMES)

Jeremiah 29:11

I know the plans that I have for you, declares the Lord. They are plans for peace and not disaster, plans to give you a future filled with hope.

(GOD'S WORD)

Encouragement

For I know the thoughts that I think toward you, saith the LORD, thoughts of peace, and not of evil, to give you an expected end.

(KING JAMES)

Lamentations 3:25-26

**The LORD is good to those who wait for him,
to anyone who seeks help from him.**

**It is good to continue to hope and wait silently
for the LORD to save us.**

(GOD'S WORD)

The LORD is good unto them that wait for him, to the soul that seeketh him.

It is good that a man should both hope and quietly wait for the salvation of the LORD.

(KING JAMES)

2 Corinthians 4:16-18

That is why we are not discouraged. Though outwardly we are wearing out, inwardly we are renewed day by day. Our suffering is light and temporary and is producing for us an eternal glory that is greater than anything we can imagine. We don't look for things that can be seen but for things that can't be seen. Things that can be seen are only temporary. But things that can't be seen last forever.

(GOD'S WORD)

For which cause we faint not; but though our outward man perish, yet the inward man is renewed day by day.

For our light affliction, which is but for a moment, worketh for us a far more exceeding and eternal weight of glory;
While we look not at the things which are seen, but at the things which are not seen: for the things which are seen are temporal; but the things which are not seen are eternal.

(KING JAMES)

2 Thessalonians 2:16-17

God our Father loved us and by his kindness gave us everlasting encouragement and good hope. Together with our Lord Jesus Christ, may he encourage and strengthen you to do and say everything that is good.

(GOD'S WORD)

Now our Lord Jesus Christ himself, and God, even our Father, which hath loved us, and hath given us everlasting consolation and good hope through grace,
Comfort your hearts, and stablish you in every good word and work.

(KING JAMES)

Encouragement

Hebrews 10:24

We must also consider how to encourage each other to show love and to do good things.

(GOD'S WORD)

And let us consider one another to provoke unto love and to good works.

(KING JAMES)

1 Peter 5:10

God, who shows you his kindness and who has called you through Christ Jesus to his eternal glory, will restore you, strengthen you, make you strong, and support you as you suffer for a little while.

(GOD'S WORD)

But the God of all grace, who hath called us unto his eternal glory by Christ Jesus, after that ye have suffered a while, make you perfect, stablish, strengthen, settle you.

(KING JAMES)

Father's Day

Exodus 20:12

Honor your father and your mother, so that you may live for a long time in the land the LORD your God is giving you.

(GOD'S WORD)

Father's Day

Honour thy father and thy mother: that thy days may be long upon the land which the LORD thy God giveth thee.

(KING JAMES)

Psalm 103:13

**As a father has compassion for his children,
so the LORD has compassion for those who fear him.**

(GOD'S WORD)

Like as a father pitieth his children, so the LORD pitieth them that fear him.

(KING JAMES)

Proverbs 17:6

**Grandchildren are the crown of grandparents,
and parents are the glory of their children.**

(GOD'S WORD)

Children's children are the crown of old men; and the glory of children are their fathers.

(KING JAMES)

I Thessalonians 3:11-12

We pray that God our Father and the Lord Jesus will guide us to you. We also pray that the Lord will greatly increase your love for each other and for everyone else, just as we love you.

(GOD'S WORD)

Now God himself and our Father, and our Lord Jesus Christ, direct our way unto you.

And the Lord make you to increase and abound in love one toward another, and toward all men, even as we do toward you.

(KING JAMES)

Father's Day

Hebrews 12:1-3

Since we are surrounded by so many examples ⌊of faith⌋, we must get rid of everything that slows us down, especially sin that distracts us. We must run the race that lies ahead of us and never give up. We must focus on Jesus, the source and goal of our faith. He saw the joy ahead of him, so he endured death on the cross and ignored the disgrace it brought him. Then he received the highest position in heaven, the one next to the throne of God. Think about Jesus, who endured opposition from sinners, so that you don't become tired and give up.

(GOD'S WORD)

Wherefore seeing we also are compassed about with so great a cloud of witnesses, let us lay aside every weight, and the sin which doth so easily beset us, and let us run with patience the race that is set before us,

Looking unto Jesus the author and finisher of our faith; who for the joy that was set before him endured the cross, despising the shame, and is set down at the right hand of the throne of God.

For consider him that endured such contradiction of sinners against himself, lest ye be wearied and faint in your minds.

(KING JAMES)

Friendship

1 Samuel 18:1

David finished talking to Saul. After that, Jonathan became David's closest friend. He loved David as much as ⌊he loved⌋ himself.

(GOD'S WORD)

And it came to pass, when he had made an end of speaking unto Saul, that the soul of Jonathan was knit with the soul of David, and Jonathan loved him as his own soul.

(KING JAMES)

Psalm 133:1

See how good and pleasant it is
when brothers and sisters live together in harmony!

(GOD'S WORD)

Behold, how good and how pleasant it is for brethren to dwell together in unity!

(KING JAMES)

Friendship

Proverbs 17:17

A friend always loves,
and a brother is born to share trouble.

(GOD'S WORD)

A friend loveth at all times, and a brother is born for adversity.

(KING JAMES)

Proverbs 18:24

Friends can destroy one another,
but a loving friend can stick closer than family.

(GOD'S WORD)

A man that hath friends must shew himself friendly: and there is a friend that sticketh closer than a brother.

(KING JAMES)

Proverbs 27:6

Wounds made by a friend are intended to help,
but an enemy's kisses are too much to bear.

(GOD'S WORD)

Faithful are the wounds of a friend; but the kisses of an enemy are deceitful.

(KING JAMES)

Proverbs 27:9

Perfume and incense make the heart glad,
but the sweetness of a friend is a fragrant forest.

(GOD'S WORD)

Friendship

Ointment and perfume rejoice the heart: so doth the seetness of a man's
friend by hearty counsel.

(KING JAMES)

Proverbs 27:17

As iron sharpens iron,
so one person sharpens the wits of another.

(GOD'S WORD)

Iron sharpeneth iron; so a man sharpeneth the countenance of his friend.
(KING JAMES)

Ecclesiastes 4:10

If one falls, the other can help his friend get up. But how tragic it is
for the one who is all alone when he falls. There is no one to help
him get up.

(GOD'S WORD)

For if they fall, the one will lift up his fellow: but woe to him that is alone
when he falleth; for he hath not another to help him up.

(KING JAMES)

John 15:13

The greatest love you can show is to give your life for your friends.
(GOD'S WORD)

Greater love hath no man than this, that a man lay down his life for
his friends.

(KING JAMES)

Friendship

Romans 12:10

Be devoted to each other like a loving family. Excel in showing respect for each other.

(GOD'S WORD)

Be kindly affectioned one to another with brotherly love; in honour preferring one another.

(KING JAMES)

1 Corinthians 13:4-8a

Love is patient. Love is kind. Love isn't jealous. It doesn't sing its own praises. It isn't arrogant. It isn't rude. It doesn't think about itself. It isn't irritable. It doesn't keep track of wrongs. It isn't happy when injustice is done, but it is happy with the truth. Love never stops being patient, never stops believing, never stops hoping, never gives up.

Love never comes to an end.

(GOD'S WORD)

Charity suffereth long, and is kind; charity envieth not; charity vaunteth not itself, is not puffed up,

Doth not behave itself unseemly, seeketh not her own, is not easily provoked, thinketh no evil;

Rejoiceth not in iniquity, but rejoiceth in the truth;

Beareth all things, believeth all things, hopeth all things, endureth all things.

Charity never faileth.

(KING JAMES)

Philippians 4:1

So, brothers and sisters, I love you and miss you. You are my joy and my crown. Therefore, dear friends, keep your relationship with the Lord firm!

(GOD'S WORD)

Therefore, my brethren dearly beloved and longed for, my joy and crown, so stand fast in the Lord, my dearly beloved.

(KING JAMES)

Get Well

∞

1 Chronicles 16:11

Search for the Lord and his strength.
Always seek his presence.

(GOD'S WORD)

Seek the Lord and his strength, seek his face continually.

(KING JAMES)

Psalm 27:14

Wait with hope for the Lord.
Be strong, and let your heart be courageous.
Yes, wait with hope for the Lord.

(GOD'S WORD)

Wait on the LORD: be of good courage, and he shall strengthen thine heart: wait, I say, on the LORD.

(KING JAMES)

Psalm 34:18

The LORD is near to those whose hearts are humble.
He saves those whose spirits are crushed.

(GOD'S WORD)

The LORD is nigh unto them that are of a broken heart; and saveth such as be of a contrite spirit.

(KING JAMES)

Psalm 42:5

Why are you discouraged, my soul?
Why are you so restless?
  Put your hope in God,
    because I will still praise him.
      He is my savior and my God.

(GOD'S WORD)

Why are thou cast down, O my soul? and why art thou disquieted in me? hope thou in God: for I shall yet praise him for the help of his countenance.

(KING JAMES)

Psalm 54:4

God is my helper!
The Lord is the provider for my life.

(GOD'S WORD)

Behold, God is mine helper: the Lord is with them that uphold my soul.

(KING JAMES)

Get Well

Psalm 55:22

**Turn your burdens over to the LORD,
and he will take care of you.
He will never let the righteous person stumble.**

(GOD'S WORD)

Cast thy burden upon the LORD, and he shall sustain thee: he shall never suffer the righteous to be moved.

(KING JAMES)

Psalm 68:19

**Thanks be to the Lord,
who daily carries our burdens for us.
God is our salvation.**

(GOD'S WORD)

Blessed be the Lord, who daily loadeth us with benefits, even the God of our salvation.

(KING JAMES)

Psalm 103:2-3

**Praise the LORD, my soul,
and never forget all the good he has done:
He is the one who forgives all your sins,
the one who heals all your diseases.**

(GOD'S WORD)

Bless the LORD, O my soul, and forget not all his benefits:

Who forgiveth all thine iniquities; who healeth all thy diseases.

(KING JAMES)

Get Well

Psalm 116:7

**Be at peace again, my soul,
because the LORD has been good to you.**

(GOD'S WORD)

Return unto thy rest, O my soul; for the LORD hath dealt bountifully with thee.

(KING JAMES)

Proverbs 17:22

**A joyful heart is good medicine,
but depression drains one's strength.**

(GOD'S WORD)

A merry heart doeth good like a medicine: but a broken spirit drieth the bones.

(KING JAMES)

3 John 2

Dear friend, I know that you are spiritually well. I pray that you're doing well in every other way and that you're healthy.

(GOD'S WORD)

Beloved, I wish above all things that thou mayest prosper and be in health, even as thy soul prospereth.

(KING JAMES)

Good Friday

Isaiah 53:5

He was wounded for our rebellious acts.
He was crushed for our sins.
He was punished so that we could have peace,
and we received healing from his wounds.

(GOD'S WORD)

But he was wounded for our transgressions, he was bruised for our iniquities: the chastisement of our peace was upon him; and with his stripes we are healed.

(KING JAMES)

Mark 15:39

When the officer who stood facing Jesus saw how he gave up his spirit, he said, "Certainly, this man was the Son of God!"

(GOD'S WORD)

And when the centurion, which stood over against him, saw that he so cried out, and gave up the ghost, he said, Truly this man was the Son of God.

(KING JAMES)

Luke 23:46

Jesus cried out in a loud voice, "Father, into your hands I entrust my spirit." After he said this, he died.

(GOD'S WORD)

And when Jesus had cried with a loud voice, he said, Father, into thy hands I commend my spirit: and having said thus, he gave up the ghost.

(KING JAMES)

Luke 24:7

He said, "The Son of Man must be handed over to sinful people, be crucified, and come back to life on the third day."

(GOD'S WORD)

Saying, The Son of man must be delivered into the hands of sinful men, and be crucified, and the third day rise again.

(KING JAMES)

2 Corinthians 5:21

God had Christ, who was sinless, take our sin so that we might receive God's approval through him.

(GOD'S WORD)

For he hath made him to be sin for us, who knew no sin; that we might be made the righteousness of God in him.

(KING JAMES)

Good Friday

Colossians 1:19-20

God was pleased to have all of himself live in Christ. God was also pleased to bring everything on earth and in heaven back to himself through Christ. He did this by making peace through Christ's blood sacrificed on the cross.

(GOD'S WORD)

For it pleased the Father that in him should all fulness dwell;

And, having made peace through the blood of his cross, by him to reconcile all things unto himself; by him, I say, whether they be things in earth, or things in heaven.

(KING JAMES)

Hebrews 2:9

Jesus was made a little lower than the angels, but we see him crowned with glory and honor because he suffered death. Through God's kindness he died on behalf of everyone.

(GOD'S WORD)

But we see Jesus, who was made a little lower than the angels for the suffering of death, crowned with glory and honour; that he by the grace of God should taste death for every man.

(KING JAMES)

1 Peter 2:24

Christ carried our sins in his body on the cross so that freed from our sins, we could live a life that has God's approval. His wounds have healed you.

(GOD'S WORD)

Who his own self bare our sins in his own body on the tree, that we, being dead to sins, should live unto righteousness: by whose stripes ye were healed.

(KING JAMES)

Graduation

2 Samuel 22:31

God's way is perfect!
 The promise of the LORD has proven to be true.
  He is a shield to all those who take refuge in him.

(GOD'S WORD)

As for God, his way is perfect; the word of the LORD is tried: he is a buckler to all them that trust in him.

(KING JAMES)

1 Chronicles 16:11

Search for the LORD and his strength.
Always seek his presence.

(GOD'S WORD)

Seek the LORD and his strength, seek his face continually.

(KING JAMES)

Graduation

Psalm 54:4

**God is my helper!
The Lord is the provider for my life.**

(GOD'S WORD)

Behold, God is mine helper: the Lord is with them that uphold my soul.

(KING JAMES)

Psalm 90:12

**Teach us to number each of our days
    so that we may grow in wisdom.**

(GOD'S WORD)

So teach us to number our days, that we may apply our hearts unto wisdom.

(KING JAMES)

Psalm 111:10

**The fear of the LORD is the beginning of wisdom.
Good sense is shown by everyone
    who follows ⌊God's guiding principles⌋.
His praise continues forever.**

(GOD'S WORD)

The fear of the LORD is the beginning of wisdom: a good understanding have all they that do his commandments: his praise endureth for ever.

(KING JAMES)

Psalm 118:8

**It is better to depend on the LORD
    than to trust mortals.**

(GOD'S WORD)

Graduation

It is better to trust in the LORD than to put confidence in man.

(KING JAMES)

Psalm 119:165
There is lasting peace for those who love your teachings.
  Nothing can make those people stumble.

(GOD'S WORD)

Great peace have they which love thy law: and nothing shall offend them.

(KING JAMES)

Proverbs 3:5-6
Trust the LORD with all your heart,
  and do not rely on your own understanding.
In all your ways acknowledge him,
  and he will make your paths smooth.

(GOD'S WORD)

Trust in the LORD with all thine heart; and lean not unto thine own understanding.

In all thy ways acknowledge him, and he shall direct thy paths.

(KING JAMES)

Proverbs 4:23
Guard your heart more than anything else,
  because the source of your life flows from it.

(GOD'S WORD)

Keep thy heart with all diligence; for out of it are the issues of life.

(KING JAMES)

Graduation

Proverbs 16:3

**Entrust your efforts to the Lord,
and your plans will succeed.**

(GOD'S WORD)

Commit thy works unto the Lord, and thy thoughts shall be established.
(KING JAMES)

Ecclesiastes 11:9

You young people should enjoy yourselves while you're young. You should let your hearts make you happy when you're young. Follow wherever your heart leads you and whatever your eyes see. But realize that God will make you give an account for all these things when he judges everyone.

(GOD'S WORD)

Rejoice, O young man, in thy youth; and let thy heart cheer thee in the days of thy youth, and walk in the ways of thine heart, and in the sight of thine eyes: but know thou, that for all these things God will bring thee into judgment.

(KING JAMES)

Matthew 6:33-34

**But first, be concerned about his kingdom and what has his approval. Then all these things will be provided for you.
So don't ever worry about tomorrow. After all, tomorrow will worry about itself. Each day has enough trouble of its own.**

(GOD'S WORD)

But seek ye first the kingdom of God, and his righteousness; and all these things shall be added unto you.

Take therefore no thought for the morrow: for the morrow shall take thought for the things of itself. Sufficient unto the day is the evil thereof.

(KING JAMES)

1 Corinthians 2:9

But as Scripture says:

"No eye has seen,
 no ear has heard,
  and no mind has imagined
   the things that God has prepared
    for those who love him."

(GOD'S WORD)

But as it is written, Eye hath not seen, nor ear heard, neither have entered into the heart of man, the things which God hath prepared for them that love him.

(KING JAMES)

2 Timothy 3:14-15

However, continue in what you have learned and found to be true. You know who your teachers were. From infancy you have known the Holy Scriptures. They have the power to give you wisdom so that you can be saved through faith in Christ Jesus.

(GOD'S WORD)

But continue thou in the things which thou hast learned and hast been assured of, knowing of whom thou hast learned them;

And that from a child thou hast known the holy scriptures, which are able to make thee wise unto salvation through faith which is in Christ Jesus.

(KING JAMES)

Grandparent's Day

2 Samuel 22:31

God's way is perfect!
  The promise of the LORD has proven to be true.
    He is a shield to all those who take refuge in him.

(GOD'S WORD)

As for God, his way is perfect; the word of the LORD is tried: he is a buckler to all them that trust in him.

(KING JAMES)

Psalm 116:7

Be at peace again, my soul,
  because the LORD has been good to you.

(GOD'S WORD)

Return unto thy rest, O my soul; for the LORD hath dealt bountifully with thee.

(KING JAMES)

Grandparent's Day

Psalm 128:5-6

May the Lord bless you from Zion
** so that you may see Jerusalem prospering**
**   all the days of your life.**
May you live to see your children's children.

Let there be peace in Israel!

(GOD'S WORD)

The Lord shall bless thee out of Zion: and thou shalt see the good of
Jerusalem all the days of thy life.

Yea, thou shalt see thy children's children, and peace upon Israel.

(KING JAMES)

Proverbs 16:31

Silver hair is a beautiful crown found in a righteous life.

(GOD'S WORD)

The hoary head is a crown of glory, if it be found in the way of
righteousness.

(KING JAMES)

Proverbs 17:6

Grandchildren are the crown of grandparents,
** and parents are the glory of their children.**

(GOD'S WORD)

Children's children are the crown of old men; and the glory of children are
their fathers.

(KING JAMES)

Letter to Father or Mother

Psalm 103:13

**As a father has compassion for his children,
  so the Lord has compassion for those who fear him.**

(GOD'S WORD)

Like as a father pitieth his children, so the Lord pitieth them that fear him.

(KING JAMES)

Proverbs 11:16

**A gracious woman wins respect,
  but ruthless men gain riches.**

(GOD'S WORD)

A gracious woman retaineth honour: and strong men retain riches.

(KING JAMES)

Proverbs 17:6

**Grandchildren are the crown of grandparents,
  and parents are the glory of their children.**

(GOD'S WORD)

Children's children are the crown of old men; and the glory of children are
their fathers.

(KING JAMES)

1 Thessalonians 3:11-12

We pray that God our Father and the Lord Jesus will guide us to you. We also pray that the Lord will greatly increase your love for each other and for everyone else, just as we love you.

(GOD'S WORD)

Now God himself and our Father, and our Lord Jesus Christ, direct our way unto you.

And the Lord make you to increase and abound in love one toward another, and toward all men, even as we do toward you.

(KING JAMES)

Letter to Son or Daughter

1 Chronicles 16:11

**Search for the LORD and his strength.
Always seek his presence.**

(GOD'S WORD)

Seek the LORD and his strength, seek his face continually.

(KING JAMES)

1 Chronicles 28:9

And you, my son Solomon, learn to know your father's God. Serve the LORD wholeheartedly and willingly because he searches every heart and understands every thought ⌊we have⌋. If you dedicate your life to serving him, he will accept you. But if you abandon him, he will reject you from then on.

(GOD'S WORD)

And thou, Solomon my son, know thou the God of thy father, and serve him with a perfect heart and with a willing mind: for the LORD searcheth all hearts, and understandeth all the imaginations of the thoughts: if thou seek him, he will be found of thee; but if thou forsake him, he will cast thee off for ever.

(KING JAMES)

Psalm 118:8

**It is better to depend on the LORD
than to trust mortals.**

(GOD'S WORD)

It is better to trust in the LORD than to put confidence in man.

(KING JAMES)

Psalm 119:9

**How can a young person keep his life pure?
⌊He can do it⌋ by holding on to your word.**

(GOD'S WORD)

Wherewithal shall a young man cleanse his way? by taking heed thereto according to thy word.

(KING JAMES)

Psalm 143:10

**Teach me to do your will, because you are my God.
May your good Spirit lead me on level ground.**

(GOD'S WORD)

Teach me to do thy will; for thou art my God: thy spirit is good; lead me into the land of uprightness.

(KING JAMES)

Proverbs 1:8

**My son,
  listen to your father's discipline,
    and do not neglect your mother's teachings.**

(GOD'S WORD)

My son, hear the instruction of thy father, and forsake not the law of thy mother.

(KING JAMES)

Proverbs 1:10

**My son,
  if sinners lure you, do not go along.**

(GOD'S WORD)

My son, if sinners entice thee, consent thou not.

(KING JAMES)

Proverbs 4:23

**Guard your heart more than anything else,
  because the source of your life flows from it.**

(GOD'S WORD)

Keep thy heart with all diligence; for out of it are the issues of life.

(KING JAMES)

Proverbs 11:16

A gracious woman wins respect,
but ruthless men gain riches.

(GOD'S WORD)

A gracious woman retaineth honour: and strong men retain riches.

(KING JAMES)

Proverbs 20:11

Even a child makes himself known by his actions,
whether his deeds are pure or right.

(GOD'S WORD)

Even a child is known by his doings, whether his work be pure, and whether it be right.

(KING JAMES)

Proverbs 23:22

Listen to your father since you are his son,
and do not despise your mother because she is old.

(GOD'S WORD)

Hearken unto thy father that begat thee, and despise not thy mother when she is old.

(KING JAMES)

Proverbs 27:11

Be wise, my son, and make my heart glad
so that I can answer anyone who criticizes me.

(GOD'S WORD)

My son, be wise, and make my heart glad, that I may answer him that reproacheth me.

(KING JAMES)

Proverbs 31:30

Charm is deceptive, and beauty evaporates,
₍but₎ a woman who has the fear of the LORD should be praised.

(GOD'S WORD)

Favour is deceitful, and beauty is vain: but a woman that feareth the LORD, she shall be praised.

(KING JAMES)

Ecclesiastes 12:1

Remember your Creator when you are young,
before the days of trouble come
and the years catch up with you.
They will make you say,
"I have found no pleasure in them."

(GOD'S WORD)

Remember now thy Creator in the days of thy youth, while the evil days come not, nor the years draw nigh, when thou shalt say, I have no pleasure in them.

(KING JAMES)

Letter to Son or Daughter

Jeremiah 29:11

I know the plans that I have for you, declares the Lord. They are plans for peace and not disaster, plans to give you a future filled with hope.

(GOD'S WORD)

For I know the thoughts that I think toward you, saith the Lord, thoughts of peace, and not of evil, to give you an expected end.

(KING JAMES)

Romans 12:2

Don't become like the people of this world. Instead, change the way you think. Then you will always be able to determine what God really wants—what is good, pleasing, and perfect.

(GOD'S WORD)

And be not conformed to this world: but be ye transformed by the renewing of your mind, that ye may prove what is that good, and acceptable, and perfect, will of God.

(KING JAMES)

1 Timothy 4:12

Don't let anyone look down on you for being young. Instead, make your speech, behavior, love, faith, and purity an example for other believers.

(GOD'S WORD)

Let no man despise thy youth; but be thou an example of the believers, in word, in conversation, in charity, in spirit, in faith, in purity.

(KING JAMES)

2 Timothy 2:1

My child, find your source of strength in the kindness of Christ Jesus.

(GOD'S WORD)

Thou therefore, my son, be strong in the grace that is in Christ Jesus.

(KING JAMES)

2 Timothy 2:22

Stay away from lusts which tempt young people. Pursue what has God's approval. Pursue faith, love, and peace together with those who worship the Lord with a pure heart.

(GOD'S WORD)

Flee also youthful lusts: but follow righteousness, faith, charity, peace, with them that call on the Lord out of a pure heart.

(KING JAMES)

2 Timothy 3:14-15

However, continue in what you have learned and found to be true. You know who your teachers were. From infancy you have known the Holy Scriptures. They have the power to give you wisdom so that you can be saved through faith in Christ Jesus.

(GOD'S WORD)

But continue thou in the things which thou hast learned and hast been assured of, knowing of whom thou hast learned them;

And that from a child thou hast known the holy scriptures, which are able to make thee wise unto salvation through faith which is in Christ Jesus.

(KING JAMES)

Mother's Day

1 John 2:28

Now, dear children, live in Christ. Then, when he appears we will have confidence, and when he comes we won't turn from him in shame.

(GOD'S WORD)

And now, little children, abide in him; that, when he shall appear, we may have confidence, and not be ashamed before him at his coming.

(KING JAMES)

3 John 4

Nothing makes me happier than to hear that my children are living according to the truth.

(GOD'S WORD)

I have no greater joy than to hear that my children walk in truth.

(KING JAMES)

Mother's Day

Exodus 20:12

Honor your father and your mother, so that you may live for a long time in the land the LORD your God is giving you.

(GOD'S WORD)

Mother's Day

Honour thy father and thy mother: that thy days may be long upon the land which the LORD thy God giveth thee.

(KING JAMES)

Psalm 78:4

**We will not hide them from our children.
We will tell the next generation
about the LORD's power and great deeds
and the miraculous things he has done.**

(GOD'S WORD)

We will not hide them from their children, shewing to the generation to come the praises of the LORD, and his strength, and his wonderful works that he hath done.

(KING JAMES)

Proverbs 11:16

**A gracious woman wins respect,
but ruthless men gain riches.**

(GOD'S WORD)

A gracious woman retaineth honour: and strong men retain riches.

(KING JAMES)

Proverbs 17:6

**Grandchildren are the crown of grandparents,
and parents are the glory of their children.**

(GOD'S WORD)

Children's children are the crown of old men; and the glory of children are their fathers.

(KING JAMES)

New Year's

Proverbs 31:30-31

Charm is deceptive, and beauty evaporates,
₍but₎ a woman who has the fear of the LORD should be praised.
Reward her for what she has done,
and let her achievements praise her at the city gates.

(GOD'S WORD)

Favour is deceitful, and beauty is vain: but a woman that feareth the LORD, she shall be praised.

Give her of the fruit of her hands; and let her own works praise her in the gates.

(KING JAMES)

New Year's

∞

Psalm 90:12

Teach us to number each of our days
so that we may grow in wisdom.

(GOD'S WORD)

So teach us to number our days, that we may apply our hearts unto wisdom.

(KING JAMES)

Psalm 111:10

The fear of the Lord is the beginning of wisdom.
Good sense is shown by everyone
who follows ⌊God's guiding principles⌋.
His praise continues forever.

(GOD'S WORD)

The fear of the Lord is the beginning of wisdom: a good understanding
have all they that do his commandments: his praise endureth for ever.

(KING JAMES)

Psalm 119:165

There is lasting peace for those who love your teachings.
Nothing can make those people stumble.

(GOD'S WORD)

Great peace have they which love thy law: and nothing shall offend them.

(KING JAMES)

Proverbs 3:5-6

Trust the Lord with all your heart,
and do not rely on your own understanding.
In all your ways acknowledge him,
and he will make your paths smooth.

(GOD'S WORD)

Trust in the Lord with all thine heart; and lean not unto thine own
understanding.

In all thy ways acknowledge him, and he shall direct thy paths.

(KING JAMES)

New Year's

Proverbs 16:3

**Entrust your efforts to the LORD,
and your plans will succeed.**

(GOD'S WORD)

Commit thy works unto the LORD, and thy thoughts shall be established.
(KING JAMES)

1 Thessalonians 5:23-24

**May the God who gives peace make you holy in every way. May he
keep your whole being—spirit, soul, and body—blameless when
our Lord Jesus Christ comes. The one who calls you is faithful, and
he will do this.**

(GOD'S WORD)

And the very God of peace sanctify you wholly; and I pray God your whole
spirit and soul and body be preserved blameless unto the coming of our
Lord Jesus Christ.

Faithful is he that calleth you, who also will do it.

(KING JAMES)

Jude 24-25

**God can guard you so that you don't fall and so that you can be full
of joy as you stand in his glorious presence without fault. Before
time began, now, and for eternity glory, majesty, power, and
authority belong to the only God, our Savior, through Jesus Christ
our Lord. Amen.**

(GOD'S WORD)

Now unto him that is able to keep you from falling, and to present you faultless before the presence of his glory with exceeding joy,

To the only wise God our Saviour, be glory and majesty, dominion and power, both now and ever. Amen.

(KING JAMES)

Retirement

2 Samuel 22:31

God's way is perfect!
  The promise of the Lord has proven to be true.
    He is a shield to all those who take refuge in him.

(GOD'S WORD)

As for God, his way is perfect; the word of the Lord is tried: he is a buckler to all them that trust in him.

(KING JAMES)

Psalm 115:1

Don't give glory to us, O Lord.
Don't give glory to us.
  Instead, give glory to your name
    because of your mercy and faithfulness.

(GOD'S WORD)

Retirement

Not unto us, O LORD, not unto us, but unto thy name give glory, for thy mercy, and for thy truth's sake.

(KING JAMES)

Psalm 116:7

Be at peace again, my soul,
 because the LORD has been good to you.

(GOD'S WORD)

Return unto thy rest, O my soul; for the LORD hath dealt bountifully with thee.

(KING JAMES)

Psalm 119:165

There is lasting peace for those who love your teachings.
Nothing can make those people stumble.

(GOD'S WORD)

Great peace have they which love thy law: and nothing shall offend them.

(KING JAMES)

Proverbs 16:3

Entrust your efforts to the LORD,
 and your plans will succeed.

(GOD'S WORD)

Commit thy works unto the LORD, and thy thoughts shall be established.

(KING JAMES)

Galatians 6:9-10

We can't allow ourselves to get tired of living the right way. Certainly, each of us will receive ⌊everlasting life⌋ at the proper time, if we don't give up. Whenever we have the opportunity, we have to do what is good for everyone, especially for the family of believers.

(GOD'S WORD)

And let us not be weary in well doing: for in due season we shall reap, if we faint not.

As we have therefore opportunity, let us do good unto all men, especially unto them who are of the household of faith.

(KING JAMES)

Philippians 4:6-7

Never worry about anything. But in every situation let God know what you need in prayers and requests while giving thanks. Then God's peace, which goes beyond anything we can imagine, will guard your thoughts and emotions through Christ Jesus.

(GOD'S WORD)

Be careful for nothing; but in every thing by prayer and supplication with thanksgiving let your requests be made known unto God.

And the peace of God, which passeth all understanding, shall keep your hearts and minds through Christ Jesus.

(KING JAMES)

Secretary's Day

Hebrews 11:1

Faith assures us of things we expect and convinces us of the existence of things we cannot see.

(GOD'S WORD)

Now faith is the substance of things hoped for, the evidence of things not seen.

(KING JAMES)

Secretary's Day

∞

2 Samuel 22:31

God's way is perfect!
 The promise of the LORD has proven to be true.
  He is a shield to all those who take refuge in him.

(GOD'S WORD)

As for God, his way is perfect; the word of the LORD is tried: he is a buckler to all them that trust in him.

(KING JAMES)

1 Chronicles 16:11

Search for the LORD and his strength.
Always seek his presence.

(GOD'S WORD)

Secretary's Day

Seek the LORD and his strength, seek his face continually.

(KING JAMES)

Psalm 112:1

Hallelujah!

**Blessed is the person who fears the LORD
and is happy to obey his commands.**

(GOD'S WORD)

Praise ye the LORD. Blessed is the man that feareth the LORD, that delighteth greatly in his commandments.

(KING JAMES)

Proverbs 3:5-6

**Trust the LORD with all your heart,
and do not rely on your own understanding.
In all your ways acknowledge him,
and he will make your paths smooth.**

(GOD'S WORD)

Trust in the LORD with all thine heart; and lean not unto thine own understanding.

In all thy ways acknowledge him, and he shall direct thy paths.

(KING JAMES)

Proverbs 16:3

**Entrust your efforts to the LORD,
and your plans will succeed.**

(GOD'S WORD)

Thank You

Commit thy works unto the LORD, and thy thoughts shall be established.

(KING JAMES)

1 Corinthians 10:31

So, whether you eat or drink, or whatever you do, do everything to the glory of God.

(GOD'S WORD)

Whether therefore ye eat, or drink, or whatsoever ye do, do all to the glory of God.

(KING JAMES)

Colossians 3:23

Whatever you do, do it wholeheartedly as though you were working for your real master and not merely for humans.

(GOD'S WORD)

And whatsoever ye do, do it heartily, as to the Lord, and not unto men.

(KING JAMES)

Thank You

1 Chronicles 29:13

**Our God, we thank you
and praise your wonderful name.**

(GOD'S WORD)

Thank You

Now therefore, our God, we thank thee, and praise thy glorious name.

(KING JAMES)

Acts 24:3

We appreciate what you've done in every way and in every place, and we want to thank you very much.

(GOD'S WORD)

We accept it always, and in all places, most noble Felix, with all thankfulness.

(KING JAMES)

Romans 1:8

First, I thank my God through Jesus Christ for every one of you because the news of your faith is spreading throughout the whole world.

(GOD'S WORD)

First, I thank my God through Jesus Christ for you all, that your faith is spoken of throughout the whole world.

(KING JAMES)

1 Corinthians 1:4

I always thank God for you because Christ Jesus has shown you God's good will.

(GOD'S WORD)

I thank my God always on your behalf, for the grace of God which is given you by Jesus Christ.

(KING JAMES)

Thank You

2 Corinthians. 9:11

God will make you rich enough so that you can always be generous. Your generosity will produce thanksgiving to God because of us.

(GOD'S WORD)

Being enriched in every thing to all bountifulness, which causeth through us thanksgiving to God.

(KING JAMES)

Ephesians 1:16

I never stop thanking God for you. I always remember you in my prayers.

(GOD'S WORD)

Cease not to give thanks for you, making mention of you in my prayers.

(KING JAMES)

Philippians 1:3

I thank my God for all the memories I have of you.

(GOD'S WORD)

I thank my God upon every remembrance of you.

(KING JAMES)

1 Thessalonians 3:9

We can never thank God enough for all the joy you give us as we rejoice in God's presence.

(GOD'S WORD)

For what thanks can we render to God again for you, for all the joy wherewith we joy for your sakes before our God.

(KING JAMES)

Thank You

1 Thessalonians 5:18

Whatever happens, give thanks, because it is God's will in Christ Jesus that you do this.

(GOD'S WORD)

In every thing give thanks: for this is the will of God in Christ Jesus concerning you.

(KING JAMES)

Thanksgiving

Psalm 50:23

Whoever offers thanks as a sacrifice honors me.
I will let everyone who continues in my way
  see the salvation that comes from God.

(GOD'S WORD)

Whoso offereth praise glorifieth me: and to him that ordereth his conversation aright will I shew the salvation of God.

(KING JAMES)

Psalm 98:1

Sing a new song to the LORD
 because he has done miraculous things.
  His right hand and his holy arm
 have gained victory for him.

(GOD'S WORD)

O sing unto the LORD a new song; for he hath done marvellous things: his right hand, and his holy arm, hath gotten him the victory.

(KING JAMES)

Psalm 106:1

Hallelujah!

Give thanks to the LORD because he is good,
 because his mercy endures forever.

(GOD'S WORD)

Praise ye the LORD. O give thanks unto the LORD; for he is good: for his mercy endureth for ever.

(KING JAMES)

Psalm 116:7

Be at peace again, my soul,
 because the LORD has been good to you.

(GOD'S WORD)

Return unto thy rest, O my soul; for the LORD hath dealt bountifully with thee.

(KING JAMES)

Thanksgiving

Psalm 118:28

**You are my God, and I give thanks to you.
My God, I honor you highly.**

(GOD'S WORD)

Thou art my God, and I will praise thee: thou art my God, I will exalt thee.
(KING JAMES)

Colossians 2:6-7

You received Christ Jesus the Lord, so continue to live as Christ's people. Sink your roots in him and build on him. Be strengthened by the faith that you were taught, and overflow with thanksgiving.
(GOD'S WORD)

As ye have therefore received Christ Jesus the Lord, so walk ye in him:
Rooted and built up in him, and stablished in the faith, as ye have been taught, abounding therein with thanksgiving.

(KING JAMES)

1 Thessalonians 5:18

Whatever happens, give thanks, because it is God's will in Christ Jesus that you do this.

(GOD'S WORD)

In every thing give thanks: for this is the will of God in Christ Jesus concerning you.

(KING JAMES)

Thinking of You

Romans 1:11-12

I long to see you to share a spiritual blessing with you so that you will be strengthened. What I mean is that we may be encouraged by each other's faith.

(GOD'S WORD)

For I long to see you, that I may impart unto you some spiritual gift, to the end ye may be established;

That is, that I may be comforted together with you by the mutual faith both of you and me.

(KING JAMES)

Philippians 1:3-4

I thank my God for all the memories I have of you. Every time I pray for all of you, I do it with joy.

(GOD'S WORD)

I thank my God upon every remembrance of you,

Always in every prayer of mine for you all making request with joy.

(KING JAMES)

Thinking of You

Philippians 4:1

So, brothers and sisters, I love you and miss you. You are my joy and my crown. Therefore, dear friends, keep your relationship with the Lord firm!

(GOD'S WORD)

Therefore, my brethren dearly beloved and longed for, my joy and crown, so stand fast in the Lord, my dearly beloved.

(KING JAMES)

2 John 12

I have a lot to write to you. I would prefer not to write a letter. Instead, I hope to visit and talk things over with you personally. Then we will be completely filled with joy.

(GOD'S WORD)

Having many things to write unto you, I would not write with paper and ink: but I trust to come unto you, and speak face to face, that our joy may be full.

(KING JAMES)

Valentine's Day

Song of Songs 1:2

Let him kiss me with the kisses of his mouth.
  Your expressions of love are better than wine.

(GOD'S WORD)

Let him kiss me with the kisses of his mouth: for thy love is better than wine.

(KING JAMES)

Song of Songs 2:14

My dove, in the hiding places of the rocky crevices,
  in the secret places of the cliffs,
let me see your figure and hear your voice.
Your voice is sweet, and your figure is lovely.

(GOD'S WORD)

O my dove, that art in the clefts of the rock, in the secret places of the stairs, let me see thy countenance, let me hear thy voice; for sweet is thy voice, and thy countenance is comely.

(KING JAMES)

Valentine's Day

Song of Songs 4:7

You are beautiful in every way, my true love.
There is no blemish on you.

(GOD'S WORD)

Thou art all fair, my love; there is no spot in thee.

(KING JAMES)

Song of Songs 4:9-10

My bride, my sister, you have charmed me.
You have charmed me
   with a single glance from your eyes,
   with a single strand of your necklace.
How beautiful are your expressions of love, my bride, my sister!
How much better are your expressions of love than wine
   and the fragrance of your perfume than any spice.

(GOD'S WORD)

Thou hast ravished my heart, my sister, my spouse; thou hast ravished my heart with one of thine eyes, with one chain of thy neck.

How fair is thy love, my sister, my spouse! how much better is thy love than wine! and the smell of thine ointments than all spices!

(KING JAMES)

Valentine's Day

Song of Songs 8:6

Wear me as a signet ring on your heart,
as a ring on your hand.
Love is as overpowering as death.
Devotion is as unyielding as the grave.
Love's flames are flames of fire,
flames that come from the LORD.

(GOD'S WORD)

Set me as a seal upon thine heart, as a seal upon thine arm: for love is strong as death; jealousy is cruel as the grave: the coals thereof are coals of fire, which hath a most vehement flame.

(KING JAMES)

Song of Songs 8:7a

Raging water cannot extinguish love,
and rivers will never wash it away.

(GOD'S WORD)

Many waters cannot quench love, neither can the floods drown it.

(KING JAMES)

1 Corinthians 13:4-8a

Love is patient. Love is kind. Love isn't jealous. It doesn't sing its own praises. It isn't arrogant. It isn't rude. It doesn't think about itself. It isn't irritable. It doesn't keep track of wrongs. It isn't happy when injustice is done, but it is happy with the truth. Love never stops being patient, never stops believing, never stops hoping, never gives up.

Love never comes to an end.

(GOD'S WORD)

Charity suffereth long, and is kind; charity envieth not; charity vaunteth not itself, is not puffed up,

Doth not behave itself unseemly, seeketh not her own, is not easily provoked, thinketh no evil;

Rejoiceth not in iniquity, but rejoiceth in the truth;

Beareth all things, believeth all things, hopeth all things, endureth all things.

Charity never faileth.

(KING JAMES)

1 Corinthians 13:13

So these three things remain: faith, hope, and love. But the best one of these is love.

(GOD'S WORD)

And now abideth faith, hope, charity, these three; but the greatest of these is charity.

(KING JAMES)

Philippians 1:7

You have a special place in my heart. So it's right for me to think this way about all of you. All of you are my partners. Together we share God's favor, whether I'm in prison or defending and confirming the truth of the Good News.

(GOD'S WORD)

Even as it is meet for me to think this of you all, because I have you in my heart; inasmuch as both in my bonds, and in the defence and confirmation of the gospel, ye all are partakers of my grace.

(KING JAMES)

Wedding

∞

Ruth 1:16-17

But Ruth answered, "Don't force me to leave you. Don't make me turn back from following you. Wherever you go, I will go, and wherever you stay, I will stay. Your people will be my people, and your God will be my God. Wherever you die, I will die, and I will be buried there with you. May the LORD strike me down if anything but death separates you and me!"

(GOD'S WORD)

And Ruth said, Intreat me not to leave thee, or to return from following after thee: for whither thou goest, I will go; and where thou lodgest, I will lodge: thy people shall be my people, and thy God my God:

Where thou diest, will I die, and there will I be buried: the LORD do so to me, and more also, if ought but death part thee and me.

(KING JAMES)

1 Chronicles 16:11

**Search for the LORD and his strength.
Always seek his presence.**

(GOD'S WORD)

Seek the LORD and his strength, seek his face continually.

(KING JAMES)

Psalm 20:4

**He will give you your heart's desire
  and carry out all your plans.**

(GOD'S WORD)

Grant thee according to thine own heart, and fulfil all thy counsel.

(KING JAMES)

Psalm 34:3

**Praise the LORD's greatness with me.
Let us highly honor his name together.**

(GOD'S WORD)

O magnify the LORD with me, and let us exalt his name together.

(KING JAMES)

Psalm 90:12

**Teach us to number each of our days
  so that we may grow in wisdom.**

(GOD'S WORD)

So teach us to number our days, that we may apply our hearts
unto wisdom.

(KING JAMES)

Wedding

Psalm 119:165

There is lasting peace for those who love your teachings.
  Nothing can make those people stumble.

(GOD'S WORD)

Great peace have they which love thy law: and nothing shall offend them.
(KING JAMES)

Proverbs 3:5-6

Trust the LORD with all your heart,
  and do not rely on your own understanding.
In all your ways acknowledge him,
  and he will make your paths smooth.

(GOD'S WORD)

Trust in the LORD with all thine heart; and lean not unto thine own understanding.

In all thy ways acknowledge him, and he shall direct thy paths.
(KING JAMES)

Proverbs 5:18

Let your own fountain be blessed,
  and enjoy the girl you married when you were young.

(GOD'S WORD)

Let thy fountain be blessed: and rejoice with the wife of thy youth.
(KING JAMES)

Wedding

Proverbs 18:22

**Whoever finds a wife finds something good
and has obtained favor from the L**ORD**.**

(GOD'S WORD)

Whoso findeth a wife findeth a good thing, and obtaineth favour of the
LORD.

(KING JAMES)

Proverbs 19:14

**Home and wealth are inherited from fathers,
but a sensible wife comes from the L**ORD**.**

(GOD'S WORD)

House and riches are the inheritance of fathers and a prudent wife is from
the LORD.

(KING JAMES)

Ecclesiastes 4:9-10a

**Two people are better than one because ⌊together⌋ they have a good
reward for their hard work. If one falls, the other can help his
friend get up.**

(GOD'S WORD)

Two are better than one; because they have a good reward for their labour.
For if they fall, the one will lift up his fellow.

(KING JAMES)

Song of Songs 8:7a

**Raging water cannot extinguish love,
and rivers will never wash it away.**

(GOD'S WORD)

Many waters cannot quench love, neither can the floods drown it.

(KING JAMES)

Jeremiah 29:11

**I know the plans that I have for you, declares the LORD. They are
plans for peace and not disaster, plans to give you a future filled
with hope.**

(GOD'S WORD)

For I know the thoughts that I think toward you, saith the LORD, thoughts
of peace, and not of evil, to give you an expected end.

(KING JAMES)

1 Corinthians 13:4-8a

**Love is patient. Love is kind. Love isn't jealous. It doesn't sing its
own praises. It isn't arrogant. It isn't rude. It doesn't think about
itself. It isn't irritable. It doesn't keep track of wrongs. It isn't
happy when injustice is done, but it is happy with the truth. Love
never stops being patient, never stops believing, never stops
hoping, never gives up.**

Love never comes to an end.

(GOD'S WORD)

Charity suffereth long, and is kind; charity envieth not; charity vaunteth not itself, is not puffed up,

Doth not behave itself unseemly, seeketh not her own, is not easily provoked, thinketh no evil;

Rejoiceth not in iniquity, but rejoiceth in the truth;

Beareth all things, believeth all things, hopeth all things, endureth all things.

Charity never faileth.

(KING JAMES)

1 Corinthians 13:13

So these three things remain: faith, hope, and love. But the best one of these is love.

(GOD'S WORD)

And now abideth faith, hope, charity, these three; but the greatest of these is charity.

(KING JAMES)

Ephesians 5:21

Place yourselves under each other's authority out of respect for Christ.

(GOD'S WORD)

Submitting yourselves one to another in the fear of God.

(KING JAMES)

Ephesians 5:31

That's why a man will leave his father and mother and be united with his wife, and the two will be one.

(GOD'S WORD)

For this cause shall a man leave his father and mother, and shall be joined unto his wife, and they two shall be one flesh.

(KING JAMES)

Ephesians 5:33

But every husband must love his wife as he loves himself, and wives should respect their husbands.

(GOD'S WORD)

Nevertheless let every one of you in particular so love his wife even as himself; and the wife see that she reverence her husband.

(KING JAMES)

Colossians 3:18-19

Wives, place yourselves under your husbands' authority. This is appropriate behavior for the Lord's people. Husbands, love your wives, and don't be harsh with them.

(GOD'S WORD)

Wives, submit yourselves unto your own husbands, as it is fit in the Lord. Husbands, love your wives, and be not bitter against them.

(KING JAMES)

Wedding

Hebrews 13:4

Marriage is honorable in every way, so husbands and wives should be faithful to each other. God will judge those who commit sexual sins, especially those who commit adultery.

(GOD'S WORD)

Marriage is honourable in all, and the bed undefiled: but whoremongers and adulterers God will judge.

(KING JAMES)

Verses for Other Occasions

2 Samuel 22:31

God's way is perfect!
   The promise of the Lord has proven to be true.
    He is a shield to all those who take refuge in him.

(GOD'S WORD)

As for God, his way is perfect; the word of the Lord is tried: he is a buckler to all them that trust in him.

(KING JAMES)

Psalm 119:165

There is lasting peace for those who love your teachings.
  Nothing can make those people stumble.

(GOD'S WORD)

Great peace have they which love thy law: and nothing shall offend them.
(KING JAMES)

Proverbs 3:5-6

Trust the LORD with all your heart,
  and do not rely on your own understanding.
In all your ways acknowledge him,
  and he will make your paths smooth.

(GOD'S WORD)

Trust in the LORD with all thine heart; and lean not unto thine own understanding.

In all thy ways acknowledge him, and he shall direct thy paths.
(KING JAMES)

Proverbs 16:3

Entrust your efforts to the LORD,
  and your plans will succeed.

(GOD'S WORD)

Commit thy works unto the LORD, and thy thoughts shall be established.
(KING JAMES)

Romans 15:13

May God, the source of hope, fill you with joy and peace through your faith in him. Then you will overflow with hope by the power of the Holy Spirit.

(GOD'S WORD)

Now the God of hope fill you with all joy and peace in believing, that ye may abound in hope, through the power of the Holy Ghost.

(KING JAMES)

1 Corinthians 1:4

I always thank God for you because Christ Jesus has shown you God's good will.

(GOD'S WORD)

I thank my God always on your behalf, for the grace of God which is given you by Jesus Christ.

(KING JAMES)

1 Corinthians 10:31

So, whether you eat or drink, or whatever you do, do everything to the glory of God.

(GOD'S WORD)

Whether therefore ye eat, or drink, or whatsoever ye do, do all to the glory of God.

(KING JAMES)

1 Corinthians 16:13-14

Be alert. Be firm in the Christian faith. Be courageous and strong. Do everything with love.

(GOD'S WORD)

Watch ye, stand fast in the faith, quit you like men, be strong.

Let all your things be done with charity.

(KING JAMES)

2 Corinthians 5:9

Whether we live in the body or move out of it, our goal is to be pleasing to him.

(GOD'S WORD)

Wherefore we labour, that, whether present or absent, we may be accepted of him.

(KING JAMES)

Ephesians 1:15-16

I, too, have heard about your faith in the Lord Jesus and your love for all of God's people. For this reason I never stop thanking God for you. I always remember you in my prayers.

(GOD'S WORD)

Wherefore I also, after I heard of your faith in the Lord Jesus, and love unto all the saints,

Cease not to give thanks for you, making mention of you in my prayers.

(KING JAMES)

Ephesians 1:17

I pray that the glorious Father, the God of our Lord Jesus Christ, would give you a spirit of wisdom and revelation as you come to know Christ better.

(GOD'S WORD)

That the God of our Lord Jesus Christ, the Father of glory, may give unto you the spirit of wisdom and revelation in the knowledge of him.

(KING JAMES)

Ephesians 3:16-19

I'm asking God to give you a gift from the wealth of his glory. I pray that he would give you inner strength and power through his Spirit. Then Christ will live in you through faith. I also pray that love may be the ground into which you sink your roots and on which you have your foundation. This way, with all of God's people you will be able to understand how wide, long, high, and deep his love is. You will know Christ's love, which goes far beyond any knowledge. I am praying this so that you may be completely filled with God.

(GOD'S WORD)

That he would grant you, according to the riches of his glory, to be strengthened with might by his Spirit in the inner man;

That Christ may dwell in your hearts by faith; that ye, being rooted and grounded in love,

May be able to comprehend with all saints what is the breadth, and length, and depth, and height;

And to know the love of Christ, which passeth knowledge, that ye might be filled with all the fulness of God.

(KING JAMES)

Colossians 1:3

We always thank God, the Father of our Lord Jesus Christ, in our prayers for you.

(GOD'S WORD)

We give thanks to God and the Father of our Lord Jesus Christ, praying always for you.

(KING JAMES)

Colossians 2:6-7

You received Christ Jesus the Lord, so continue to live as Christ's people. Sink your roots in him and build on him. Be strengthened by the faith that you were taught, and overflow with thanksgiving.

(GOD'S WORD)

As ye have therefore received Christ Jesus the Lord, so walk ye in him:

Rooted and built up in him, and stablished in the faith, as ye have been taught, abounding therein with thanksgiving.

(KING JAMES)

Colossians 3:17

Everything you say or do should be done in the name of the Lord Jesus, giving thanks to God the Father through him.

(GOD'S WORD)

And whatsoever ye do in word or deed, do all in the name of the Lord Jesus, giving thanks to God and the Father by him.

(KING JAMES)

1 Thessalonians 3:9

We can never thank God enough for all the joy you give us as we rejoice in God's presence.

(GOD'S WORD)

For what thanks can we render to God again for you, for all the joy wherewith we joy for your sakes before our God.

(KING JAMES)

1 Thessalonians 3:12-13

We also pray that the Lord will greatly increase your love for each other and for everyone else, just as we love you. Then he will strengthen you to be holy. Then you will be blameless in the presence of our God and Father when our Lord Jesus comes with all God's holy people.

(GOD'S WORD)

And the Lord make you to increase and abound in love one toward another, and toward all men, even as we do toward you:

To the end he may stablish your hearts unblameable in holiness before God, even our Father, at the coming of our Lord Jesus Christ with all his saints.

(KING JAMES)

1 Thessalonians 5:16-18

Always be joyful. Never stop praying. Whatever happens, give thanks, because it is God's will in Christ Jesus that you do this.

(GOD'S WORD)

Rejoice evermore.

Pray without ceasing.

In every thing give thanks: for this is the will of God in Christ Jesus concerning you.

(KING JAMES)

2 Thessalonians 1:3

We always have to thank God for you, brothers and sisters. It's right to do this because your faith is showing remarkable growth and your love for each other is increasing.

(GOD'S WORD)

We are bound to thank God always for you, brethren, as it is meet, because that your faith groweth exceedingly, and the charity of every one of you all toward each other aboundeth.

(KING JAMES)

Verses for Other Occasions

2 Thessalonians 2:13

We always have to thank God for you, brothers and sisters. You are loved by the Lord and we thank God that in the beginning he chose you to be saved through a life of spiritual devotion and faith in the truth.

(GOD'S WORD)

But we are bound to give thanks alway to God for you, brethren beloved of the Lord, because God hath from the beginning chosen you to salvation through sanctification of the Spirit and belief of the truth.

(KING JAMES)

2 Thessalonians 2:16-17

God our Father loved us and by his kindness gave us everlasting encouragement and good hope. Together with our Lord Jesus Christ, may he encourage and strengthen you to do and say everything that is good.

(GOD'S WORD)

Now our Lord Jesus Christ himself, and God, even our Father, which hath loved us, and hath given us everlasting consolation and good hope through grace,

Comfort your hearts, and stablish you in every good word and work.

(KING JAMES)

Philemon 4-5

I always thank my God when I mention you in my prayers because I hear about your faithfulness to the Lord Jesus and your love for all of God's people.

(GOD'S WORD)

I thank my God, making mention of thee always in my prayers,

Hearing of thy love and faith, which thou hast toward the Lord Jesus, and toward all saints.

(KING JAMES)

Philemon 25
The good will of our Lord Jesus Christ be yours.

(GOD'S WORD)

The grace of our Lord Jesus Christ be with your spirit. Amen.

(KING JAMES)

Hebrews 11:1
Faith assures us of things we expect and convinces us of the existence of things we cannot see.

(GOD'S WORD)

Now faith is the substance of things hoped for, the evidence of things not seen.

(KING JAMES)

3 John 13-14
I have a lot to write to you. However, I would rather not write. I hope to visit you very soon. Then we can talk things over personally.

(GOD'S WORD)

I had many things to write, but I will not with ink and pen write unto thee:

But I trust I shall shortly see thee, and we shall speak face to face. Peace be to thee. Our friends salute thee. Greet the friends by name.

(KING JAMES)

Jude 2

May mercy, peace, and love fill your lives!

(GOD'S WORD)

Mercy unto you, and peace, and love, be multiplied.

(KING JAMES)

Jude 24-25

God can guard you so that you don't fall and so that you can be full of joy as you stand in his glorious presence without fault. Before time began, now, and for eternity glory, majesty, power, and authority belong to the only God, our Savior, through Jesus Christ our Lord. Amen.

(GOD'S WORD)

Now unto him that is able to keep you from falling, and to present you faultless before the presence of his glory with exceeding joy,

To the only wise God our Saviour, be glory and majesty, dominion and power, both now and ever. Amen.

(KING JAMES)

Revelation 22:21

The good will of the Lord Jesus be with all of you. Amen!

(GOD'S WORD)

The grace of our Lord Jesus Christ be with you all. Amen.

(KING JAMES)

Dates to Remember

January

1. _____
2. _____
3. _____
4. _____
5. _____
6. _____
7. _____
8. _____
9. _____
10. _____
11. _____
12. _____
13. _____
14. _____
15. _____
16. _____
17. _____
18. _____
19. _____
20. _____
21. _____
22. _____
23. _____
24. _____
25. _____
26. _____
27. _____
28. _____
29. _____
30. _____
31. _____

February

1. _____
2. _____
3. _____
4. _____
5. _____
6. _____
7. _____
8. _____
9. _____
10. _____
11. _____
12. _____
13. _____
14. _____
15. _____
16. _____
17. _____
18. _____
19. _____
20. _____
21. _____
22. _____
23. _____
24. _____
25. _____
26. _____
27. _____
28. _____
29. _____

Dates to Remember

March

1. _____
2. _____
3. _____
4. _____
5. _____
6. _____
7. _____
8. _____
9. _____
10. _____
11. _____
12. _____
13. _____
14. _____
15. _____
16. _____
17. _____
18. _____
19. _____
20. _____
21. _____
22. _____
23. _____
24. _____
25. _____
26. _____
27. _____
28. _____
29. _____
30. _____
31. _____

April

1. _____
2. _____
3. _____
4. _____
5. _____
6. _____
7. _____
8. _____
9. _____
10. _____
11. _____
12. _____
13. _____
14. _____
15. _____
16. _____
17. _____
18. _____
19. _____
20. _____
21. _____
22. _____
23. _____
24. _____
25. _____
26. _____
27. _____
28. _____
29. _____
30. _____

Dates to Remember

May

1. _____
2. _____
3. _____
4. _____
5. _____
6. _____
7. _____
8. _____
9. _____
10. _____
11. _____
12. _____
13. _____
14. _____
15. _____
16. _____
17. _____
18. _____
19. _____
20. _____
21. _____
22. _____
23. _____
24. _____
25. _____
26. _____
27. _____
28. _____
29. _____
30. _____
31. _____

June

1. _____
2. _____
3. _____
4. _____
5. _____
6. _____
7. _____
8. _____
9. _____
10. _____
11. _____
12. _____
13. _____
14. _____
15. _____
16. _____
17. _____
18. _____
19. _____
20. _____
21. _____
22. _____
23. _____
24. _____
25. _____
26. _____
27. _____
28. _____
29. _____
30. _____

Dates to Remember

July

1. _____
2. _____
3. _____
4. _____
5. _____
6. _____
7. _____
8. _____
9. _____
10. _____
11. _____
12. _____
13. _____
14. _____
15. _____
16. _____
17. _____
18. _____
19. _____
20. _____
21. _____
22. _____
23. _____
24. _____
25. _____
26. _____
27. _____
28. _____
29. _____
30. _____
31. _____

August

1. _____
2. _____
3. _____
4. _____
5. _____
6. _____
7. _____
8. _____
9. _____
10. _____
11. _____
12. _____
13. _____
14. _____
15. _____
16. _____
17. _____
18. _____
19. _____
20. _____
21. _____
22. _____
23. _____
24. _____
25. _____
26. _____
27. _____
28. _____
29. _____
30. _____
31. _____

Dates to Remember

September

1. _____
2. _____
3. _____
4. _____
5. _____
6. _____
7. _____
8. _____
9. _____
10. _____
11. _____
12. _____
13. _____
14. _____
15. _____
16. _____
17. _____
18. _____
19. _____
20. _____
21. _____
22. _____
23. _____
24. _____
25. _____
26. _____
27. _____
28. _____
29. _____
30. _____

October

1. _____
2. _____
3. _____
4. _____
5. _____
6. _____
7. _____
8. _____
9. _____
10. _____
11. _____
12. _____
13. _____
14. _____
15. _____
16. _____
17. _____
18. _____
19. _____
20. _____
21. _____
22. _____
23. _____
24. _____
25. _____
26. _____
27. _____
28. _____
29. _____
30. _____
31. _____

Dates to Remember

November

1. _____
2. _____
3. _____
4. _____
5. _____
6. _____
7. _____
8. _____
9. _____
10. _____
11. _____
12. _____
13. _____
14. _____
15. _____
16. _____
17. _____
18. _____
19. _____
20. _____
21. _____
22. _____
23. _____
24. _____
25. _____
26. _____
27. _____
28. _____
29. _____
30. _____

December

1. _____
2. _____
3. _____
4. _____
5. _____
6. _____
7. _____
8. _____
9. _____
10. _____
11. _____
12. _____
13. _____
14. _____
15. _____
16. _____
17. _____
18. _____
19. _____
20. _____
21. _____
22. _____
23. _____
24. _____
25. _____
26. _____
27. _____
28. _____
29. _____
30. _____
31. _____